Self-Di
for Writers

Writing Is Hard,

But You Too Can

Write and Publish Books Regularly

By Martin Meadows

Download Another Book for Free

I want to thank you for buying my book and offer you another book (just as valuable as this one): *Grit: How to Keep Going When You Want to Give Up*, completely free.

Visit the link below to receive it:

https://www.profoundselfimprovement.com/writers

In *Grit*, I'll tell you exactly how to stick to your goals, using proven methods from peak performers and science.

In addition to getting *Grit*, you'll also have an opportunity to get my new books for free, enter giveaways, and receive other valuable emails from me.

Again, here's the link to sign up:

https://www.profoundselfimprovement.com/writers

Table of Contents

Prologue

Once upon a time, there was a writer who could write thousands upon thousands of words a day, every single day, 365 days a year. Procrastination, writer's block, frustration, self-doubt—these words had never appeared in the writer's dictionary. Prolific as they come, this writer couldn't understand why people considered writing to be a hard job.

Three sentences in, and you can already tell that such a writer has never existed and never will. Writing is often hard and frustrating. Fortunately, there are certain strategies that every writer can use to make the process less burdensome and more effortless.

In this short book, we'll address some of the most common problems writers have including a lack of willpower to get started, procrastination, self-doubt, discouragement due to low or non-existent sales, and a lack of creative energy.

Before we start, you might be wondering: who am I to talk about all of this?

I've been writing in various forms ever since I was seven or so. I started by writing stories about fictional animals my family adopted—including a caiman (I have no idea why it was a caiman instead of a regular, more fun to be around, pet).

Recently, my primary focus has been writing personal development books. At the time of writing this, I've released eighteen books on the topic (this is the nineteenth book), with several of them becoming long-term bestsellers on Amazon.

Having written some novels and short stories (beyond my childhood career), I have experience with fiction, too, but my primary focus is non-fiction. However, most of the information in this book applies equally well to non-fiction, fiction, and any other type of writing. The principles of self-discipline for writers stay the same regardless of what you write.

When reading this book, please keep in mind that writing advice is subjective. There's no research proving that this particular method is the best way to write or that this particular strategy will increase your output by 50%.

None of the advice I present in this book is set in stone. Take what works for you, discard what doesn't, but first try whatever appeals to you so that you can form your own opinion and gain practical experience.

My target reader is a professional author, or a person who wishes to become one.

If you don't wish to make writing your career, you can benefit from this book, too, but you won't resonate with every piece of advice. Professional writers need to treat their profession more seriously than hobby writers who might be opposed to treating their passion as a job.

As a non-fiction writer in a genre known for vapid, meandering rants, I prefer brevity, so this book, like my other titles, cuts straight to the chase. You should spend more time writing than reading about writing, anyway.

You're probably getting antsy to get to the good stuff—and so am I—so let's end this introduction here and talk about the most fundamental principles of self-discipline for writers.

Chapter 1: Build Your Foundations on These Three Principles

Let's be clear before we talk about anything else: if you don't enjoy the process of writing, none of the suggestions I offer in this book will be of much use to you.

This doesn't mean that you have to love every single aspect of writing. The question comes down to: *overall* does writing give you more joy or pain? Or in other words, do you find fulfillment in writing even if it often tests your patience?

If you write because you think you *should* write but not because you *want* to write, writing is not the right choice for you as your lack of enthusiasm will creep into your work. In addition to that, if you don't enjoy something at least a little bit, you can't expect to stick to it in the long term.

If writing generally gives you more joy than pain, this book is for you. We'll learn how to make it an even more joyful activity and overcome the most common pitfalls that make writing less fun. Let's start by talking about the three basic principles that will help you write and publish consistently.

Write What You Like—But There's a Caveat

Writing goes most smoothly if you write about something that excites you. Enthusiasm is also essential to write in an engaging way. However, there's a danger in assuming that writing about what interests you will solve everything.

If you want to become a professional writer, you need an audience. The size of the audience needs to be large enough to provide good odds of success. A bestselling author Chris Fox calls this principle "writing to market."[1]

For example, as important as the topic might be, few people will be interested in reading your book about the migratory patterns of penguins. That's not to say you can't become the world's most well-known expert on penguins and earn a good living writing books about them. That's not to say that this particular topic is boring or unimportant, either.

We're looking at it only from the perspective of a person who wants to become a professional writer and enjoy a thriving career. Your odds of financial success writing about an obscure topic are lower than those of, say, an average sci-fi writer, a genre that's infinitely bigger, with millions of voracious readers.

You might be thinking: *hey, we were supposed to talk about self-discipline for writers and here you are talking about money.*

As I emphasized it in prologue, we operate under the assumption that you are or want to become a professional writer. Money is an important part of the equation if you want to make a living from writing. We writers are humans too, and humans need to have shelter, eat, and perhaps enjoy a few other things, too—and they all cost money.

It's difficult to exhibit self-discipline if you lack the basic necessities to perform the demanding job of writing. No matter how much you love writing, if nobody is reading your work and your goal is to earn from your work, you'll eventually get discouraged and lose the will to keep going. Conversely, if you're properly compensated for your work, writing is not only easier, but often more enjoyable, too. And no, expecting money from your hard work doesn't taint your reputation as an artist.

Don't feel guilty that money motivates you to write. If you want to get fit, you want your efforts to help you feel and look better. Without results, you'll struggle with self-discipline. Why would writing be any different?

That's why it's important to ensure a lot of people are interested in what you want to write, even if you don't want to make millions from your writing.

Find a topic or a genre you enjoy, and make sure that it's something many people enjoy. This leads us to two questions: how to identify what interests you and how to identify what interests other people. Let's discuss this in more detail.

How to Identify What Interests You?

Start by establishing whether you want to write fiction or non-fiction. You can determine this by taking a look at your personal library.

If you read mostly fiction, you should probably write fiction as you already understand what makes a story captivating. If you read mostly non-fiction, you'll probably have a better feel for sharing information than telling stories.

If you're unsure, try writing both fiction and non-fiction and see what excites you more and is easier. You don't have to write anything long. Compare how you feel when you write a short story and when you write a how-to article. What feels more natural to you? Can you see yourself doing this every day?

I decided to focus on non-fiction because that's what I read most often. I love learning new things and I'd rather learn specific skills than read a story. Don't get me wrong, I appreciate good stories, but my ability to tell a story isn't nearly as developed as the ability to share information. I don't feel much resistance when writing non-fiction, while writing fiction often feels like squeezing the last bit of toothpaste out of the tube.

Having said that, writers evolve and their preferences change. Perhaps you'll start out as a fiction writer only to discover that you prefer sharing information. Or maybe you'll dedicate yourself to non-fiction only to realize that you prefer the challenge of writing novels.

For now, just pick what interests you most at the moment. You can always switch later if you want. After you decide on fiction or non-fiction, it's time to decide on a specific niche or genre. What do you read about most often? What types of books or stories excite you most?

In fiction, in addition to the stories you read most often, consider what movies or TV series you watch, too. A story is a story, regardless if it's a book, a movie, a TV show or even a play.

When it comes to non-fiction, take stock of your skills, experience, and future goals, too. What do your friends or family ask you to help them with? What do you like to talk about or teach to others? Are there any topics you'd like to explore yourself and could cover your learning process in an interesting way in your book? (Yes, you can write non-fiction as a non-expert: just be clear about it and share with your readers your learning process.)

Now that you've found something that interests you, it's time to consider how many people find it relevant, too.

How to Identify What Interests Other People?

The simplest way to identify what interests other people is quick and easy.

A rule of thumb for non-fiction: if your book is about health, wealth, or happiness (this includes relationships), you're in a big market. We all want to be healthy, prosperous, and happy; it's our human nature.

A rule of thumb for fiction: if you're writing in any of the most popular genres including romance, erotica, thriller, crime, mystery, science-fiction, or fantasy, you're in a big market. You can research the size of each genre by searching for the breakdown of book sales by genre.

Obviously, the more niche you go, the size of your audience will grow smaller. If you want to make sure that you aren't in an obscure niche, you can go deeper and use my more advanced research method.

Browse through the bestseller lists on Amazon in a genre or niche that interests you.

Identify the current trends (books released in the last year or so) to discover what specific subgenres or topics are most popular now. You can capitalize on these trends by riding the wave of popularity. You can also find evergreen topics and subgenres. These are the books that have been bestsellers for many years, usually because they talk about topics that never get old or tell stories that appeal to our human nature (for example, a classic rags to riches story).

If there are at least several books on the bestseller lists that are similar to what you want to write, it's because there's a market for them. Bonus points if they have hundreds of reviews: it confirms that they have sold a lot of copies and means that they deeply resonate with their readers.

I like using Amazon for market research because it's the biggest bookstore in the world. It has about a 40% share in print books, and a staggering 83% in e-book sales.[2] If a book performs well on Amazon, it's a bestseller, period.

When researching individual titles, take a look at the Amazon Best Sellers Rank, which you can find under the product details on the book's page. Make sure that you're viewing a Kindle version of the book. You'll see something like this:

#781 Paid in Kindle Store

#5 in Motivational Self-Help (Kindle Store)

#36 in Success Self-Help

#45 in Motivational Self-Help (Books)

For the purposes of our research, the only thing that interests us is the first rank, the one that is followed by "Paid in Kindle Store." The lower the rank, the better the book sells. To give you a rough estimate, a Kindle book with a rank;

- lower than #10,000 sells at least 25 e-book copies a day, all the way up to thousands for the books in top100,

- between #10,000 and #50,000 sells 10–25 copies a day,

- between #50,000 and #100,000 sells between 1–10 copies a day,

- higher than #100,000 sells less than one copy a day.

The algorithm for the sales rank takes into account a few different factors, so these numbers are just rough estimations. Also, there are separate ranks for Kindle books, paperbacks, hardcovers, audiobooks, and any other format. These estimates are for the Kindle rankings.

Before you decide on a niche or subgenre, find at least a few similar books and check their sales ranks. To ensure that you're writing in a market that is popular enough, there should be at least a few books with a rank below #100,000, and ideally below #50,000. For the biggest odds of success—but also more competition—focus on topics and genres with books that rank below #10,000.

Read—What You Write and What You Don't Write

Writers can't exist in a vacuum. While producing your own work is the most important part of the process—otherwise you can't call yourself a writer, can you? Reading is a key aspect of your job, too.

The impact of reading on writing is similar to the impact of proper nutrition on exercise. Can you exercise without a healthy diet? Of course you can. Will you achieve your maximum potential? Highly unlikely. You need both to achieve a synergic effect.

Reading is important for a couple of reasons, all of which affect your performance as a writer:

1. Reading provides inspiration. Reading various books, not even necessarily in your own niche or genre, will expose you to new perspectives, ideas, writing styles, trends, and gaps in the market.

2. Reading recharges. As writers, we often live in our own worlds. This is good when we're in the zone and words flow smoothly, but sometimes we need to take a break from our own work to recharge our batteries. Reading provides this escape and has been proven to have a positive impact on stress levels, sleep, high self-esteem, and mental health.[3]

3. Reading helps you write better. One of the best ways to improve your writing skills is to read other books and take notes whenever a book bores you, frustrates you, or otherwise feels off.

One of the reasons why I write short, concise books is because I often get bored by long-winded self-help books with 400 pages, only 10 of which contain actual advice, with the rest discussing irrelevant theory or drawn out stories.

In the same way, you can jot down when a book captivates you and figure out why. Then ask yourself how you can apply this to your own writing, too. For example, I like non-fiction books that start with a surprising paragraph. I decided to adapt this in my own writing, too. It's fun to come up with ideas to surprise a reader from the first page—and it also breaks the initial resistance many writers have when staring at the first, blank page of a new book.

How do you find time for reading?

If you're strapped for time, put the minutes you usually waste into use. Read when waiting, commuting via public transportation, having a lunch break, or doing anything else when you otherwise waste time.

If you can't read by yourself, listen to audiobooks. This way, you'll make the most out of your daily commutes by car, doing house chores, jogging, or anything else that doesn't require your full focus.

Given that an average US adult spends nearly six hours per day watching various types of video[4], most people don't suffer from a lack of time: they suffer from a lack of clear priorities. If you want to treat writing seriously, you should prioritize reading over other ways to entertain yourself.

There's one more important reason why reading is important, but it requires a separate subchapter to cover in more detail…

Let the Rules Help You (But Don't Let Them Enslave You)

There's no better research than reading the biggest bestsellers to understand how the story is structured, what type of characters they feature, what information they convey or what tone they keep throughout the book. Building upon what works is one of the best ways to become a more efficient writer.

Outlining your book to make sure it follows the most fundamental conventions in your niche or genre can serve as a useful tool to get started. Established rules can also serve as checkpoints, guiding you throughout the process.

For example, in fiction you go from conflict to its resolution to another conflict and another resolution all the way until the end of the book. This is one of the most basic rules that, when reflected in the outline of your story, will help you write faster and with less resistance. You'll always know what comes next. This is the basis of bestselling author Randy

Ingermanson's Snowflake Method, one of the most popular methods to write a novel in an efficient way.[5]

When writing a how-to book, writing down a list of questions you want to answer will provide you with guideposts. I always start writing a book by creating its skeleton first: a list of chapters divided into subchapters covering specific aspects of a problem or providing specific solutions. When I complete the outline, all I have to do is fill in the blanks—which makes my writing sessions focused as I don't waste time asking myself what to write about.

Mastering the basic elements of successful books: book structure, tropes, archetypes, teaching methods, etc. gives you a framework upon which you can construct your own book more easily. This doesn't mean that you always need to follow the exact same template or blindly copy everything you've observed in similar books. The rules can help you, but they shouldn't enslave you by limiting your creativity.

When in doubt, defaulting to the standards is a safe bet as that's what your readers expect and enjoy. When feeling adventurous, let your creativity go wild and break the rules with a smile on your face—but accept that charting new waters comes with risks, one of which is that you might write a book that will appeal to few people.

BUILD YOUR FOUNDATIONS ON THESE THREE PRINCIPLES: QUICK RECAP

1. Writing needs to give you more joy than pain. Otherwise you're pursuing the wrong career.

2. The first principle to write and publish consistently is to write what interests you with a caveat that you need to identify a niche or a genre that has an established audience of people interested in it.

3. To identify what interests you, take a look at what types of books you read most frequently. For fiction, you can also consider what movies or TV series you watch, while for non-fiction, you can take a stock of your skills, experience, and future goals.

4. To identify what interests other people, a rule of thumb is as follows: for non-fiction, health, wealth, happiness, and relationships are all big markets. For fiction, this includes the biggest genres like romance, erotica, thriller, crime, mystery, science-fiction, or fantasy.

5. A more advanced method to identify a lucrative niche or genre is to browse through

Amazon's bestseller lists and check the sales rank of books similar to what you'd like to write. There should be at least a few books with a rank below #100,000, and ideally below #50,000. For the biggest odds of writing a big bestseller—but also more competition—focus on topics and genres with books that rank below #10,000.

6. The second principle to write and publish consistently is to read a lot. Reading provides inspiration that will help you boost your creativity. Reading is also a recharging activity that will have a positive impact on your well-being. Lastly, reading helps you write better because you can deconstruct a book you're reading to identify how to improve your own writing.

7. Find time for reading by turning time wasted waiting, commuting, having a lunch break, etc. into a daily reading practice. Don't discount audiobooks: they can help you make the most of engaging in repetitive, boring activities like commuting by car or engaging in household chores.

8. The third principle to write and publish consistently is to let the established standards and rules help you. Outlining a book and making sure that it follows a reader-friendly template, contains tropes, archetypes, teaching methods, etc. that fit your book will help you write faster. Defaulting to the common elements found in your niche or genre is safe, because that's what your readers expect and like. However, if you're feeling adventurous, don't let the rules limit your creativity—but accept the associated risks.

Chapter 2: How to Develop a Strong Work Ethic as a Writer

Stephen King writes in his book *On Writing: A Memoir of the Craft*: "Amateurs sit and wait for inspiration, the rest of us just get up and go to work."[6]

Out of all the inspirational quotes a writer could read, I find these are the most powerful words of encouragement.

What's so encouraging about them, you might wonder?

The encouragement comes from the underlying meaning of this quote: professional writing doesn't depend on some inborn traits, being blessed by the muse, or anything else you can't control. Professional writing is good old-fashioned work, period. All of us can accomplish great feats in writing if we're only willing to get up and go to work.

This leads us to the first, non-negotiable rule of disciplined writers: for most consistent results, write consistently, ideally every day.

3 Steps to a Strong Work Ethic as a Writer

The prospect of writing a book is overwhelming enough. Without any signposts—which a consistent routine provides—it's unlikely that your book idea will transform into reality anytime soon. Consistently hitting your word counts ensures steady, visible progress, which makes it easier to keep going when the inevitable doubts appear in your head.

If you want to write a novel of an average length— about 60,000 words—you can get it done in just two months if you write 1,000 words a day. This, depending on the difficulty of the project, shouldn't take you more than 2–3 hours a day.

If you don't have the luxury of 2–3 spare hours a day, how about writing 500 words? You can reach this word quota in 60–90 minutes and finish the first draft of your book in four months.

Still too much? 250 words a day, which amounts to 30–45 minutes of focused work, means that your first manuscript will be done in eight months.

To accomplish this, you need to develop a strong work ethic as a writer. Let's cover three keys to a consistent writing schedule that will help you become a more disciplined and prolific writer.

1. Commit to a daily word quota

The first step to develop a strong work ethic is to establish a target. For a writer, the most important quantifiable measure is their daily or weekly word count.

Daily word quotas force you to write every day, which helps establish momentum and result in long-term consistency. They're particularly useful for people who have a tendency to procrastinate. If you have a daily quota to meet, you don't have much time to procrastinate—it has to be done today, period.

Weekly quotas give you more flexibility. You can write more when you're feeling particularly inspired, and less when you're struggling or need to attend to other obligations.

The danger of weekly quotas is that it's easy to put off writing. On Monday, you still have six more days to meet your quota. If you fail to write on Tuesday, there are still five days left. You keep postponing work until it's Saturday, and suddenly you need to complete your weekly quota in two days.

I strongly prefer daily word quotas. They enforce daily accountability and help you write in the most consistent manner over the long term.

The only danger of daily quotas is that you're under constant pressure to perform. That's why it's best not to write as much as you can every day. Always leave something in the tank so you can maintain constant momentum without the risk of a burnout caused by pursuing an ambitious daily word count.

When I started self-publishing books, I used to write 3,000 words a day. Initially everything was going well. Carried by initial excitement, I produced a lot and the quality—for my skills back then—was good.

After a few months I burned out. The mere thought of writing made me feel sick. I needed several weeks to recover before I could write again.

Today I write at a more casual pace of about 1,000–1,500 words a day. This target still helps me publish a couple of books a year, but doesn't burn me out.

Economist Adam Smith writes in his book *The Wealth of Nations*: "The man who works so moderately as to be able to work constantly not only preserves his health the longest, but, in the course of the year, executes the greatest quantity of work."[7]

Author Alex Soojung-Kim Pang shares similar views in his book *Rest: Why You Get More Done When You Work Less*, in which he posits that ranging across different historical periods and creative fields like writing, painting, and philosophy, the optimal approach to maintain a consistent work output was to work for no more than four hours a day.[8]

My personal experience confirms these findings—four hours of creative work a day is my absolute limit. Usually I can maintain the highest quality of writing only for about two, or at most three hours a day. Anything produced after that comes with a risk of lower quality—which means more work when later editing the book.

Knowing the realistic limits to creative work, what would be a good daily word count to target?

An average writer writes somewhere between 200–1,000 words an hour, depending on the genre, the difficulty of the project, available creative energy on a given day, and a host of other factors.

Some writers consistently exceed 1,000 words an hour, and some struggle to reach even 200. From my experience, a manageable pace you can achieve on a daily basis (with some training) is in the vicinity of 400–500 words an hour. This means that an achievable daily word count target for most writers is about 2,000 words a day.

I suggest starting small, with 500–1,000 words a day, and then increase it weekly until you hit your limit—then back off a little. You might hit your limit right at 1,000, or you might go all the way to 2,000 and still feel like you can produce more each day.

Experiment and find your own pace remembering that it's better to write less, but consistently, than a lot, but eventually burn out. Also, it's better to write less, but maintain quality, than write a lot, but then have to discard most of what you write.

2. Build a strong routine

A strong routine is a writer's best friend. Unless you thrive in complete chaos and hate any kind of a structure in everyday life, a routine will help you focus and write more effectively. Conversely, constantly changing when and how you write will make it difficult to complete your project.

One of the easiest ways to develop an everyday writing schedule is to ensure that you always write at the same time. To further reinforce the routine, combine it with pre-writing cues which we'll cover in this subchapter. Lastly, there are certain tools you can use while writing to make it easier—we'll discuss them in this chapter, too.

When you combine these three things, you'll build a multi-faceted, strong habit that will help you consistently put yourself in a creative mindset, in a reliable way. Let's cover these three steps one by one.

1. Specific time

I always write in the early morning. That's when I focus most easily. People are unlikely to bother you so early, there aren't any urgent things to do, it's quiet, and your energy tank is full. Moreover, if you get your daily writing done in the early morning, you're done with your most important job before other people wake up.

If you aren't an early riser and can't perform well in the morning, consider writing at night. I advise against writing during the day because there are too many distractions around that can get you out of your creative trance. Both early mornings and late nights are the quietest periods of the day when you can most easily access your creativity and focus on your job.

Having said that, it's all a personal preference, and my preferences don't have to mirror yours.

Some writers—particularly extroverts who recharge around other people—create their best work in a busy café full of people. They need the external energy to channel creativity.

Then there are your stereotypical introverts who do their best work in a quiet office with doors closed, headphones on, and a "keep out, introvert on property" sign (just kidding, my fellow introverts). To them, writing with other people around is impossible.

Experiment with different approaches. Once you find a period of time that works for you best, ensure that all, or at least most of your writing sessions happen during this time—this is your magical hour that will help you write consistently.

2. Pre-writing cues

I always make tea before I start my writing session. It's my cue to get started, and it helps me stay focused while writing.

For you, it might be coffee, a brief yoga session, a light breakfast, or maybe something more peculiar like putting on your favorite t-shirt. Developing positive triggers that put you in the writing mood will help you stave off procrastination.

There's one more pre-writing cue to help you get started. It's different than the previous triggers, though, because you do it at the end of your writing session the day before, and not immediately before your next session. Namely, when you're about to end your writing for the day, stop in the middle of a sentence so...

Sorry for my immature joke. When you're about to end your writing for the day, stop in the middle of a sentence so that the next day you'll start writing immediately. One unfinished thought often leads to another. Before you know it, thanks to this pre-writing cue you'll be well on your way to meet your word count for the day.

A similar strategy is to leave the easy parts for the hard days. For example, I sometimes leave my quick chapter recaps for a day when writing feels more difficult than usual. Since they require little creativity (all I do is summarize the points I made in the chapter), they serve as a great warm-up for a writing session.

Any type of a pre-writing cue that is healthy (no candy bars, cigarettes, or alcohol to kickstart your writing session), enjoyable, and easily replicable will help you grease the wheels of your creativity.

Think of it as creating a recipe for a productive writing session. Make sure you start at the right time. Put yourself in the writing mood with some pre-writing cues. And then the final step: learn how to optimize your writing sessions for maximum performance.

3. Tools to optimize your writing performance

One of the best tools to increase your writing output is **working in blocks of time**. I usually write in 25-minute blocks followed by a 5 or 10-minute break (loosely based on a productivity method called The Pomodoro Technique).

This way, it's easier to maintain focus. You're never more than 25 minutes away from a break, during which you can indulge in any distraction that strikes your fancy. I also find it easier to get started, knowing that I'm not about to begin a long, exhausting, two or three-hour session, but just a brief 25-minute one.

In addition to that, taking a break every 20–30 minutes is key to a healthy workplace hygiene, which is of utmost importance for any writer who doesn't want their job to ruin their health. Mobility expert Kelly Starrett emphasizes in his book *Deskbound: Standing Up to a Sitting World* that frequent movement is essential not only for your body, but also for your brain whose performance decreases with inactivity.[9]

Engaging in a few quick exercises during your break can help you stay productive for longer. You'll refocus, re-energize your body, and avoid crippling back pain that will ruin your work ethic more successfully than a premiere of a new season of your favorite TV series.

The most important thing to make this strategy work is to be honest with yourself. During your writing session, write. During your break, take a break. Don't mix the two.

If you can't write during your 25-minute block, just stare at the screen, a wall, or a window until you come up with something. Write gibberish if it helps you. Remember, you can indulge in distractions during your break. The writing block is for writing or at least trying to write.

When in doubt, follow one of my favorite maxims provided by novelist and screenwriter Raymond Chandler: "Either write or nothing... I find it works. Two very simple rules, a: you don't have to write. b: you can't do anything else. The rest comes of itself."[10]

Ideally, you would take regular breaks during every session. However, sometimes you might find yourself in the zone, with words flowing on the page as if by magic. When you're completely absorbed in the task and can effortlessly maintain concentration, don't be afraid to break the break-taking rule. Don't interrupt the magic with breaks you don't need—keep going until the magic is gone.

Another tool to help you keep writing is **introducing some playfulness**. It can be as simple as inserting some jokes in your book, creating fun and quirky characters, adapting alliterations as an attractive aspect of your writing, or any other creative measure to keep writing enjoyable.

Writing, even if you're working on a serious book for serious readers, doesn't need to be dull. Even a bland topic can be palatable if you make an effort to provide it in a more digestible way.

You can also play productivity games against yourself. For example, measure how many words you can write in each 25-minute block and try to beat your high score while maintaining the high quality of your writing.

Lastly, **music (or its lack thereof) is a powerful tool**. If you focus more easily with music, then experiment with different genres and playlists to identify what type of music helps you write most. Sing along if it helps you (though perhaps skip this one if you're writing in a public space).

If music distracts you, then embrace total silence. Ensure that your work environment is as quiet as possible—close the door, close the windows (if possible), and perhaps invest in noise-canceling headphones (or wear good earplugs) to tune out the world around you.

If you stay engaged when writing, your readers will be more interested in reading your works, too. If you feel bored, your book will reflect it, too.

3. Resist the Temptation to Edit While Writing

Editing must *not* be a part of your daily writing process. This is one of the worst mistakes you can make, so please read the next paragraphs carefully—it's that important.

When you start editing while you're supposed to be writing, it's easy to get sucked into a Mariana Trench deep hole of self-criticism and self-doubt.

Editing involves questioning every single word, sentence, and paragraph. You don't edit with your writer hat on: you edit with your disapproving and nitpicking self. If you take on both roles while you're supposed to be writing, your editor side will thwart the creativity of your writing persona.

I often find my first draft ugly. And that's okay, because that's what editing is for: polishing your rough work into a diamond. But you can't have a beautiful shiny diamond if you don't dig out a rough lump first.

Change little things here and there if it's necessary for continuity, but whenever you find yourself spending more time tinkering than writing, it's time to stop, refocus, and let the words flow smoothly without judgment. There will be time to fix bad grammar, typos, wrong word choices, arguments that don't make sense, dialogues that sound stiff, etc. When writing, write—without any filters that hamper your creativity and slow down your writing.

Where does research fit into all of this? Just like editing, any type of time-consuming research should be a separate task in which you engage outside of your writing sessions. If you have a rough outline of what you want to write on a given day, you can plan ahead and research beforehand.

If you have to conduct research while writing, focus on finding the information you need and get back to writing. If you catch yourself reading something out of curiosity instead of necessity, bookmark it and return to it during your break.

What If I Don't Hit
My Daily Word Count?

Don't panic. Don't berate yourself.

You won't always meet your daily writing targets. Life is unpredictable. You may get sick. You may get buried under unexpected work obligations. Your dog may eat your first manuscript. Things outside your control will happen.

If I miss a day, I remind myself that **it's fine to skip one day as long as you don't skip two**. One day is an exception. Two days might set a precedent.

It doesn't necessarily mean that everything is lost if you don't hit your target for a couple of days in a row. Writing should be one of the priorities for a professional writer, but sometimes it needs to fade in the background so you can tend to other, more important obligations.

If possible, try to write even just a sentence or two a day. This way, you'll maintain a semblance of momentum that will help you pick up the pace once you're ready to write full-time again.

Do I Need to Write Every Single Day Even If I Don't Have a Project to Work On?

Professional authors write for a specific purpose: they want to publish a book. To create a final product, at one point you'll have to switch your daily writing routine to a daily editing routine.

This means that instead of writing, you'll spend your time changing, reorganizing, or removing unnecessary words, sentences, paragraphs, or even entire chapters. It's an important job that requires your undivided attention.

When I'm editing the first draft of my new book, I rarely work on another book. I prefer to progress as quickly as possible with my manuscript and then give my full attention to the new project.

For me, editing is one of the most enjoyable parts of the writing process. I don't mind spending a few days to a few weeks solely dedicating my focus to editing my books.

If you don't like editing, this might be different for you. Perhaps you'll need to boost your motivation to keep editing by looking forward to your writing session later during the day.

HOW TO DEVELOP A STRONG WORK ETHIC AS A WRITER: QUICK RECAP

1. The first step to a strong work ethic as a writer is to commit to a daily word quota. Daily quotas are better than the weekly ones because they help you maintain momentum and prevent procrastination.

2. Think of writing as a marathon. It's better to write a little, but every day, than a lot, but in a sporadic fashion. A sustainable pace is somewhere around 1,000 to 2,000 words a day. Start with a lower word count and increase your pace until it gets challenging. Then back off a little to find your sweet spot that you can maintain over the long term.

3. The second step to a strong work ethic is a writing routine. This includes writing at the same time every day, pre-writing cues (tiny habits you engage in before writing to put yourself in the writing mood), and techniques to help you while you're writing (like working in blocks of time, entertaining yourself when writing, and listening to music or working in complete silence).

4. The third step to a strong work ethic is resisting the temptation to edit while writing. Editing involves questioning everything, while when you're writing, the words should flow onto the page without any judgments. With these two roles in conflict, it's impossible to write productively if you're constantly tinkering with your first draft.

5. It's okay to skip one day of writing as long as you don't skip two. If you're temporarily strapped for time, try to write just a sentence or two to maintain a semblance of momentum.

6. If you're done with the first draft of your book, don't worry about writing for the sake of writing. Focus on editing your manuscript and publishing your book. After all, that's your primary goal as a professional writer.

Chapter 3: How to Deal With Self-Doubt

If you lack confidence in yourself, you'll struggle with self-discipline. After all, how are you supposed to trust the process if you don't trust yourself? How likely are you to write consistently if you don't believe that you can make it as a writer?

Self-trust and proper, empowering beliefs, are indispensable to develop self-discipline and write consistently. That's why in this chapter we'll address some of the most common manifestations of self-doubt among writers.

1. Self-doubt Before You Even Start

"There are so many great books out there. What's the point of writing my own book?"

People who dream about writing a book but never get around to do it frequently suffer from this limiting belief. They fail to realize a few important things and consequently, sabotage themselves even before they start. Let's break this issue down into three main beliefs and how to change them to overcome this type of self-doubt.

Belief #1: There's too much competition.

It's difficult to find recent data on how many books have been published during the human history, but it's definitely *a lot*.

Google Books puts the number at 129,864,880, but this number comes from 2010 and doesn't include many self-published works.[11]

According to various statistics, at least 2 million books are released each year around the world,[12] but this number is also at least a few years old and doesn't include many self-published books.

It's safe to say that the book publishing world is indeed a crowded space. However, this should have no impact on you for three important reasons:

1. Books come and go. People love to read the most recent bestsellers. This means that you primarily compete against books released in the last few months or years—not every single book that was ever released.

Yes, there are countless classics published decades, hundreds, or thousands of years ago, but it doesn't change the fact that people still read recently released books.

In non-fiction, everybody wants the latest information. In many niches, a bestseller from two decades ago might not be relevant anymore. That's where you can step in and provide up-to-date information or a modern take on the topic.

In fiction, many people want to read the book everyone's currently raving about. Then there are also new, previously unexplored trends in fiction, which means that there's always a gap in the market for a disciplined fiction writer.

2. If there's competition, it means there's strong demand. I'd worry more about writing a book in a genre without competitors than a book in a popular, crowded niche.

If a niche is uncompetitive, there's probably a good reason why: few people are interested in the topic. As we've already discussed, professional writers should write to market. After all, we want many people reading our books, right?

Competition is also useful because it helps you improve as a writer. You have to do your best to stand out among a sea of similar books. Since the bar is set up higher, you'll grow more than if there were no competition. There's a reason why professional surfers flock to Hawaii or why some of the world's most successful entrepreneurs live in the Silicon Valley.

3. There's always a market for a new book in a genre or niche that interests people. One of the most beautiful things about humans is that we're all unique. No matter how crowded your niche or genre is and how many books you're competing with, your book will always be different because it's yours—and there's nobody else like you in the world.

There are thousands of self-help books, many of which are written by reputable scientists, professional athletes, public speakers, and other high-profile people. I'm nobody compared to them. Yet, my books are still selling and get positive reviews. Why is that so? It's because I simply provide a different point of view that resonates with some people. Your perspective is just as unique and needed in your target market as is mine.

In fiction, even if you follow the general standards of your genre, you can still inject into the story your personality, quirks, and style. Enthusiastic readers are always looking for a new, fresh voice, and the voice they're waiting for might be your very own.

Belief #2: My book won't be as great as the bestsellers.

If you're new to writing, or anything else for that matter, you won't be great at it. It's a fact of life. My first books were horrible, yet I still published them. Surprise: my world didn't end. Surprise number two: some people actually *enjoyed* those books.

You'll get better with each new book given that you actually finish it and publish it. Keeping your works unpublished is a safe choice for those who want to avoid criticism, but it won't help you develop confidence in your writing skills. And without confidence, there's no self-discipline, either.

Think of your readers: you probably have some unique insights or a story they would enjoy reading. They don't care that you aren't as great of a writer as one of your idols. All that matters to them is that you let them read your unique story or learn from you and get to know your unique point of view.

Your writing skills aren't the primary factor influencing how successful you'll be. I know some authors who have exceptional technical skills, yet sell few books compared to some bestselling, widely-acclaimed authors whose writing skills are atrocious (I don't think I need to give you any examples).

This isn't to say that you have a free pass to break every rule of good writing. This is only to emphasize that people are often willing to overlook imperfections as long as you tell a great story, explain information well, or otherwise resonate with your readers on a deep level.

I read bestselling authors published by major publishing houses and self-published authors with crude writing skills. As long as I get what I'm looking for, I'm happy to support both.

Belief #3: I have only one chance to write a perfect book.

No, you don't. You have as many chances as you want. If your book fails, few people will read it. You can unpublish it, rework it, and publish it again as a second edition. Or better yet, write it off and focus on a new book.

You're doing a disservice to your readers by trying to make your book as perfect as possible. Your readers would rather read an almost perfect book than wait for a perfect book that never comes out.

If you want to test the waters, consider using a pseudonym.

Pen names let you experiment with different genres and niches without ending up with a confusing catalog of unrelated works and books you might be embarrassed about in the future (if you're doing your best with every project, you should never be embarrassed about your work, though). Since you aren't using your real name, you're also less likely to endlessly tinker with your book, censor yourself or otherwise filter your thoughts, afraid of people judging you.

Overnight successes are rare. If you take a look at the list of the bestselling authors, you'll notice that a great majority of them have released more than a few books, often in addition to countless unpublished manuscripts or books released under other pseudonyms.

This will be most likely your experience, too—so don't wait for ages to start writing your first book, because if you want to become a professional author, your first book will most certainly not be your last.

2. Self-Doubt Due to Your Background

No matter what your background is, there's surely at least one successful author who beat the odds. Let's address some common reasons for self-doubt due to your background and why they shouldn't affect your decision to become a professional writer.

1. Age

Some people doubt they can become professional writers because they consider themselves too old. There's nothing further from the truth. Your age can be an asset. You have more real-world experience and more stories to tell.

Moreover, professional writing isn't like professional sports where your age, genes, and other factors you can't control play a big role. What matters most in writing is your dedication to the process. Your age has no impact on how determined and disciplined you can be to make your dreams come true.

2. Race or nationality

Most readers care primarily about the story you want to tell or the information you want to share. Few care what your race or nationality is—and if this has an impact on their reading choices, these are the type of readers you don't want to have anyway.

As with age, your race or nationality can be an asset, too. You might have a different perspective on things. You might resonate more with certain readers and become a leading figure in your chosen genre or niche. Or you can simply not worry about any of it at all: focus on doing your most important job instead of worrying about factors beyond your control.

3. Gender

I don't like and don't agree with the outdated, erroneous notions that only women should write romance or that only men should write thrillers. Yet, there's no denying the fact that readers expect certain things from certain genres, and unfortunately many of them are still accustomed to the long-established standards.

The tendency is slowly changing, but at the moment it's still a factor that influences your odds of success. One way to make this a non-issue is to change your gender by using a pen name. For example, J. K. Rowling became Robert Galbraith to establish herself in crime fiction.

I myself decided to use a female pen name for some (bad) romance novels I wrote in the (distant) past as I noticed that there were virtually no male names in this genre.

I don't believe that gender is such a big factor in non-fiction unless you write about gender-specific issues. For example, a male fitness expert, no matter how vast his knowledge is, probably won't resonate with women as much as a female expert who understands the needs of her audience on a more visceral level.

In any other gender-neutral niche, don't worry about your gender: we need both male and female perspectives.

4. Formal education

Education has no impact on your odds of success as a fiction writer. Thanks to the Internet, you can research whatever you need to include in your story and make it credible.

Non-fiction is different as in some niches you do require formal education to be qualified to talk about the topic. For example, if you wanted to learn how to build bridges, you'd probably want to read a book written by an engineer.

Likewise, certain subtopics in niches that otherwise don't require you to be a certified expert require formal education.

For example, as a self-help writer I emphasize it over and over again that I'm not trained to give advice about mental health issues. For that, you need a therapist. What I offer my readers is my own perspective, my own ideas, my own research, and my own personal stories. I write my books as a regular guy to resonate with a certain subgroup of self-help readers. I don't play a formal expert because I'm not one.

Your lack of formal education in the field doesn't have to be a cause for self-doubt, as long as you're ethical, clear with your readers about your background, and stick to topics that don't require formal qualification.

3. Self-doubt of an Impatient Writer

Let's imagine you're trekking through a desert.

You start at an oasis. You're well-fed, hydrated, rested, with ample supplies. The first day goes well. The second day starts to get monotonous. The next day is even more challenging. As you continue the journey, things get progressively harder. You have less and less water. Food is getting scarce. You're tired of removing scorpions from your shoes and looking out for snakes burrowed in the sand. You see an oasis on the horizon only to realize that it's a mirage.

Eventually, you lose confidence that the sandy dunes will ever end. Things are so bleak that you contemplate what it will be like to die in the desert. Will anybody ever find your body? Unbeknownst to you, as you're considering surrender, the edges of the desert are just a couple of hours away. The promised land of abundant water, food, and shade is finally within your reach—if you only keep pushing for a little while longer.

If you're wondering why I'm giving you this crazy talk, let me explain why: writing often feels as hopeless as a desert journey. That's what most writers have to go through. Most likely you won't be any different.

Before you start writing a book, tell yourself that things will be hard but you absolutely can't stop. During the journey, focus on the next immediate step (hitting your daily word count) instead of thinking too much ahead. Step by step, you'll eventually finish your project. When in doubt, remember that as long as you're moving forward, you're getting closer to your destination even it it's nowhere in sight yet.

4. Self-doubt When Editing Your Book

One of the most important rules to follow when it comes to editing is that you should always give yourself at least two weeks before you start fixing your first manuscript.

You need a fresh set of eyes to be able to spot mistakes, smooth out your writing, and look at your work from a more objective perspective. You're most emotional about your book right after you complete it. If you start editing right after you finish your book, you'll go in one of two equally bad directions:

- you'll love your manuscript so much that you'll fail to spot how many improvements it needs. This results in self-doubt when you receive your manuscript back from the professional editor, with so many corrections your eyes will bleed.

- you'll hate your manuscript so much that you'll decide to shelve your book indefinitely.

That's why it pays to take a break from your manuscript and return to it when it no longer has such an emotional impact on you. That's when you'll be able to self-edit effectively, without losing confidence in your work.

A good way to deal with self-doubt when editing is to pretend that you're editing the work of somebody else. In a sense, that's what you're doing: you're editing the work of a writer you were when you worked on a given project.

If you find this idea too esoteric, assume the job of a sculptor. Your manuscript has some great parts and some not so good parts. Focus on taking things away to let the great parts shine more brightly. Your manuscript will turn into a beautiful sculpture not by gluing new parts to it, but by removing what's unnecessary and uncovering the shape inside.

When you're done with self-editing, delegate the final editing to a professional editor you trust. An editor can do a great job only if you trust their abilities instead of questioning every comment and correction.

If you still have doubts about the quality of your book, find some beta readers to give you feedback before you conclude your project. Barring compulsively obsessive perfectionists, this approach to editing will help you create the best book you possibly can while keeping self-doubt at bay.

5. Self-doubt Associated With Publishing Your Work

The moment has come. All your background work is done, and it's time to share your final product with the world. You're dead afraid of criticism, putting off your launch date, justifying it with the need for some additional edits that never end.

There are few, if any, writers, who don't question their abilities even when they take great efforts to write the best book possible. It's scary to share your work with the world and expose yourself to criticism. It's understandable that you're tempted to avoid it, but ultimately, every artist needs to publish their works so that other people can enjoy it (and others can hate it).

One of the most paradigm-shifting thoughts I've ever heard when it comes to self-doubt and a fear of criticism are the words of Stephen King who said: "If you disapprove, I can only shrug my shoulders. It's what I have."[13]

It's what I have. What a beautiful self-assertive attitude.

Glance through your book one more time. Remember how much time and energy you invested in it. Remind yourself how hard the process was and congratulate yourself for how brave you were to endure it. Time to end this chapter in your life and share your work. And then start it all over again with another book.

HOW TO DEAL WITH SELF-DOUBT: QUICK RECAP

1. One of the most common manifestations of self-doubt are the limiting beliefs that there's too much competition, that your book won't be as great as the bestsellers, and that you have only one chance to make your book perfect.

2. To overcome the first limiting belief, remember that books come and go. Many readers prefer to read new books over those already released some time ago. This means that there's always a market for a new book. Secondly, if there's competition, it means there's strong demand. Lastly, each writer is unique and can provide fresh stories, ideas and perspectives.

3. To overcome the second limiting belief, remember that readers are often willing to overlook imperfections as long as you do your best to tell a great story or share information in a clear or entertaining way. Your technical abilities do play a role, but it's only one of the factors, not a defining one.

4. To overcome the third limiting belief, remember that overnight successes are rare. It's better to publish an imperfect book than waste years endlessly tinkering with it in exchange for a marginal improvement most readers wouldn't notice anyway.

5. Don't let your background become a cause for self-doubt. Your age, race or nationality are not important factors, and can be assets. Your gender might play a role when writing fiction. To solve this problem, you can use a pen name of a gender common in the genre. In non-fiction, your gender isn't that big of a factor unless you write about gender-specific issues. Your formal education only has an impact on writing if you want to write non-fiction about topics that do require you to be a qualified expert. If you aren't one, stick to topics that don't require formal knowledge and always be clear with your readers about your background.

6. Writing requires a lot of patience. To avoid losing hope that you'll ever finish your book, remember that every writer goes through the same difficulties you face. Focus on your next step—hitting

your daily word count—and don't think too much ahead.

7. Wait at least two weeks before you start editing your book. Otherwise you might approach it too emotionally and either overlook the glaring mistakes or be too critical of your work. Remember that self-editing can only take you so far. It will be the professional editing that will turn your manuscript into a final, polished product.

8. It's normal to be afraid to publish your book. It's a scary moment, but isn't it the very moment you've been working so hard to reach? It's time to complete a chapter of your life and share your work with the world. Remember the words of Stephen King: "If you disapprove, I can only shrug my shoulders. It's what I have."

Chapter 4: 7 Tips on How to Manage Your Energy as a Writer

Writing is hard work. It requires immense focus and creativity—day in, day out. You can't tune out while writing: you always have to be on if you want to deliver a great story or share information in a clear, entertaining way.

Writing is also stressful. Writers experience stress when they're staring at a blank page, uncertain how to begin. They feel stress when they're planning a story or outlining a non-fiction book and wondering if they'll be able to finish it. They deal with stress worrying about critics, trying to make their books perfect, or processing the fact that the book they spent months working on failed to sell many copies.

Managing your energy as a writer is vital if you want to continuously improve your skills and grow your career. Let's talk about the seven most important tips to keep you charged up and consistently hit your daily word counts.

1. Prioritize Health

Your physical and mental health affect your energy the most. Consequently, it only makes sense to prioritize health in your life—otherwise you won't be able to perform well as a human being, let alone a writer. A lot of factors contribute to your overall health, but the four fundamentals are:

1. Your diet

The foods you put in your mouth have a direct impact on your health and energy levels. If you're tired, your brain performance is compromised, too, which impairs your writing abilities.

We aren't going to start a never-ending discussion on the healthiest diet. It doesn't matter what specific diet you follow as long as it's a diet that prioritizes the foods we were designed to eat as humans: whole foods like vegetables or fruits over highly-processed junk with thirty lab-engineered ingredients.

If you're struggling with your diet, in my book *Self-Disciplined Dieter* I give tips on how to develop more self-discipline to optimize this aspect of your life.

Depending on when you write, experiment with different types of foods to find the nutrition habits that most positively impact your writing. Most likely, a light meal will be the best option to sustain your energy while writing.

You can also consider writing fasted. Research suggests that intermittent fasting might be beneficial for healthy brain aging.[14] Many followers of intermittent fasting report increased focus while fasted—me included. Obviously, anecdotal evidence doesn't carry the same weight as strict scientific studies, but it might be worth investigating to see what kind of an impact intermittent fasting has on you (please consult your physician first).

Don't forget about proper hydration. Even mild dehydration can make you feel tired or sleepy.[15] Have a glass of water or another healthy beverage within reach.

What about coffee or tea? Caffeine is considered to be a productivity booster, but research provides conflictive conclusions.

One meta-analysis shows that tea constituents L-theanine and epigallocatechin gallate, consumed alone or in combination with caffeine, improved alertness, attention, and the ability to switch between different tasks.[16] On the other hand, excessive consumption may lead to anxiety and impair sleep.[17] Some studies also suggest that caffeine can cramp creativity because we're most creative when we let our minds wander: a mental state that caffeine prevents.[18]

Overall, there are both benefits and drawbacks associated with caffeine. Research suggests that controlled consumption of caffeine in safe amounts of up to three to four cups a day is more likely to benefit health than harm.[19] Just remember that caffeine has a disruptive effect on sleep and it shouldn't be consumed less than six hours prior to bedtime.[20]

The definite answer whether caffeine is worth it depends on how you use it. If you drink more than several cups of coffee just to get through the day, then perhaps you should consider reducing your consumption. If you limit your consumption to your writing sessions and can get by without caffeine as your primary energy source, your habit is probably more beneficial than harmful.

I drink Pu-Erh tea during almost every writing session as I've trained myself to associate it with writing and use it as a cue to get to work. However, outside of early mornings I usually don't drink any other caffeinated beverages.

2. Your physical activity

Regular physical activity is natural to human beings. Unfortunately, the modern comforts made a lot of us so lazy that we barely move—and eventually pay for it dearly with nagging pains, limited range of motion, obesity, and a host of other unpleasant conditions.

Regular physical activity is even more important for professional writers—particularly those who work in a seated, unhealthy position that stresses their necks, shoulders, backs, hips, wrists—or actually, the entire body, as we aren't designed to sit in a chair for prolonged periods of time (for a great explanation why, read *Deskbound* by Kelly Starrett).

Consider standing up while writing or alternate between working in a standing and seated position. Physical inactivity not only impairs your body, but also your brain, so if you're spending a lot of time in a passive, sitting position, you're inhibiting your writing performance. The transition to a standing desk is uncomfortable, but the long-term benefits of sitting less and moving more are worth it.

Regular exercise provides another benefit for writers: the endorphin rush you feel during and after a good workout will help you relax. With a clear mind, it's easier to access creativity and write more efficiently.

I strongly suggest engaging in sports and activities that require intense focus. In addition to physical benefits, they provide a meditative experience that will improve your ability to concentrate on a single task. Some examples of such sports include any sport with instant negative consequences if you lose attention: martial arts, tennis, rock climbing, surfing, or skiing.

If you lack self-discipline to exercise regularly, read my book *How to Build Self-Discipline to Exercise* for tips on how to make exercise a habit you'll enjoy.

Experiment with exercise before you start your writing session. I often find the writing sessions I engage in after a swimming workout to be more productive than the ones I begin without any type of physical exercise beforehand. Even brief, light activity can help maintain concentration and increase productivity.

3. Your sleep

Not getting enough sleep is by far one of the worst things you can do to yourself.

Studies suggest that chronic restriction of sleep to six hours or less produces the same decrease in the cognitive performance as up to two nights of total sleep deprivation.[21] This means that even if you consistently sleep slightly less than you should, your performance is still seriously impaired.

Sleep is so important that if you need to choose between hitting your daily word count or getting adequate sleep, you should choose sleep. Overworking your body without proper recovery will eventually catch up with you—and then you won't hit your daily word counts at all.

4. Your habits

The habits you engage in most often have a big impact on your health. Any negative habits like smoking, drinking excessive alcohol or taking drugs ruin not only your body, but can also affect your writing career. Embrace habits that boost your happiness and productivity, not habits that bring you misery and cut your life short.

Yes, there are plenty of examples of writers who indulged in vices throughout their entire careers, but those careers were often cut short by premature death or interrupted by periods in which the writers struggled to regain control over their lives.

One of such examples is Stephen King who abused alcohol and drugs to such an extent that he was drunk while delivering the eulogy at his mother's funeral and barely remembered writing one of his books, *Cujo*.[22]

Upon hitting rock bottom and debating suicide, Stephen eventually got clean with the help of his wife. If it weren't for quitting his unhealthy habits, his flourishing career might have ended in the late 80s and there would be no *Green Mile*, the finished *Dark Tower* series, his must-read memoir and how-to book *On Writing*, and many other bestselling books.

There's nothing attractive in being an artist struggling with addiction. It might make a good story, but it's terrible for the person—and their family and friends—suffering from it. As a writer, you have a gift to share with the world. Take care of your health so you can consistently make the lives of other people better through your stories or non-fiction books.

2. Know Your Why

Why are you a writer? What does writing mean to you? Knowing the answer will help you gather energy to keep going when you encounter obstacles or suffer from crushing failures.

For example, writing is for me a therapeutic activity. In addition to all the tangible benefits it provides—like being able to make a living doing it—it helps me organize my thoughts, share my ideas with the world, and sometimes even solve my own problems. By writing to you, my dear reader, I also partly write to myself. I also enjoy the act of writing, including editing my books and trying to present my thoughts as clearly as possible.

Knowing what kind of internal rewards you get from writing will help you persevere when the going gets tough. Without some kind of an intrinsic compensation, you'll find it impossible to write consistently.

Your "why" can also be your "who,"—the audience that you serve with your books or your family that you can support thanks to your writing skills. Helping my parents financially was one of my original, strongest motivators to become a professional writer. Who can benefit from your writing?

3. Don't Talk Too Much About Your Book

To maintain energy while working on a new project, it's a good policy to avoid talking too much about it. If you discuss your book with others while it's not ready yet, they'll probably provide their own ideas that might clash with your own.

Seeking constructive feedback is a good idea, but getting it too early might bring confusion. This will sap you of creative energy and lead to what I call "writing to please"—filtering yourself in an effort to appeal to a certain person with whom you discussed your project.

Create a one-sentence description of your new project. If anyone asks you what you're writing, share only this quick description and don't share any specific details that would lead to discussions. This way, you'll conserve your energy instead of wasting it defending your project or considering ideas that would intrude on your personal style.

4. Work on One Project at a Time

Working on only one project at once is a safe strategy for quick progress. If you're working on one novel, it might take you, say, two months to finish the first draft. If you alternate between two different novels, it will take you four months to finish them.

Focusing on one project is energizing because you can see progress every day. When you have one project, you can dedicate your entire brainpower to this one book alone—and that will help you push through plateaus and see the project through more quickly.

The slower your progress is—and it's cut *by half* if you work on two books—the higher the risk of losing patience, getting exhausted, or developing self-doubt that will all jeopardize your projects.

I consider each new book a mini-chapter in my life, written in a voice specific to that project. Alternating between two projects—particularly if they're of a similar nature, such as two stories in the same subgenre or two how-to books on the same topic—poses a risk that they'll sound too similar to each other.

Granted, some people do well when they switch their focus, so that switching from one book to another makes them better writers. If you feel you gravitate toward this approach, experiment with it. If, however, you tend to lose your interest and focus if you're spread too thin, limit yourself to one project.

5. Capture Fleeting Ideas

When you feel particularly inspired, writing is a breeze. It feels like you're not using any energy at all: words just appear on the page and keep flowing. Great ideas are what kickstart legendary writing sessions, while the dearth of them makes writing a slog.

Remember that as a writer, you're on all the time. You might have completed your daily word quota in the morning, but your brain is always running. A great idea can strike you anywhere, anytime. That's why it's crucial to capture your fleeting ideas so you have fodder for your next writing session.

If there's any specific place, time or a situation in which great ideas strike you most often, make sure that it's a part of your routine. For example, if you often feel inspired out in nature, spend time outdoors as often as possible—and carry a notepad or keep your phone handy, ready to jot down your ideas. Next time you're writing, you'll be thankful that you capitalized on your moment of genius.

6. Don't Read Your Reviews

This might sound illogical. After all, to improve as a writer you should read your reviews to learn what people like and don't like about your books, right? That's not exactly true.

Reviews are primarily for readers, not authors. They help potential readers make a decision whether they should invest their time and money into a given book or skip it.

The thing about reviews is that they're never objective. Some readers will love your book, and some will hate it. I'm yet to find a book with universally positive reviews. Even some of the best books I've ever read have negative reviews.

Most readers aren't writers. The reason why they didn't like your book might be because they didn't like a specific character or expected a different ending. This has nothing to do with your writing skills—it's just a reader's personal preference, and you can't cater to them all.

If you're seeking feedback to improve, negative reviews should, *theoretically,* be useful. Unfortunately, a great majority of negative reviews are written by people working through their personal issues. They review the author and not the book, or post a venomous review for the sake of hurting someone for fun.

There might be some valuable feedback in *some* negative reviews, but generally speaking, they'll hurt you more than they'll help you. The negativity bias makes things of a negative nature more powerful emotionally than the positive things.[23] This means that no matter how many positive reviews of your book you'll read, if there's one bad review, that's the one you'll remember the most—and that's the one that will erode your confidence and steal your energy.

Also, book reviews often appear months or years after the book's publication date. After such a period of time, they aren't of much use anymore since you've already turned the page and probably published another, better, book.

How can you improve as a writer if you don't read your reviews, then? You learn through reading and writing a lot. You learn by getting feedback from your editor. It's impossible not to improve if you focus on these fundamentals.

For additional constructive feedback that won't discourage you, seek beta readers. Ideally, your beta readers are writers, too, or at least read a lot. They should be capable of providing feedback of an objective nature and offer it with pure intentions—to help you publish the best book you're capable of writing.

Once your book is published, you don't control how the audience reacts to it. The best you can do is start working on a new project.

7. Be Kind to Yourself

Last but definitely not least, remember that writing is a hard job and that you shouldn't be too tough on yourself when you're failing with your writing goals. We're all human beings, and human beings are imperfect. We like to strive for perfection, but we shouldn't hate ourselves if we make mistakes.

If you're struggling to gather energy to write another book or finish your current project, don't be afraid to take an extended break. Taking your mind off writing and doing something else—hanging out with your friends, engaging in your favorite hobbies, traveling, or just being lazy is important for self-care and longevity as a writer.

Seeking support and interacting with other writers can be valuable, too—sometimes only a fellow writer can understand your struggles and offer you encouragement to help you keep going.

7 TIPS ON HOW TO MANAGE YOUR ENERGY AS A WRITER: QUICK RECAP

1. If there's one thing that affects your energy as a writer the most, it's your health. The four lifestyle elements that contribute the most to your health are diet, physical activity, sleep, and other regular habits. Prioritize health to optimize your performance as a writer and ensure a long, happy career.

2. Identify the reasons why you're are a writer (including the people who benefit from your writing) and remind yourself of them when you're lacking motivation.

3. Don't talk too much about the book you're writing. It might lead to self-doubt or writing to please a person with whom you discussed your unfinished book instead of following your vision.

4. When you work on one book at a time, you're most effective. Spreading yourself over a few projects dramatically slows you down and might sap you of energy to finish any of them.

5. Good ideas can appear in your head out of the blue. Capture them immediately. Capitalizing on your moments of genius will help you write with more ease later on.

6. There's little to be gained from reading your reviews. Positive reviews might inspire you, but just one negative review can undermine your self-confidence. If you want constructive feedback, rely on your editor. You can also find beta readers who will help you perfect your book before you publish it. Once the book is on the market, the reception is out of your hands.

7. Writing is tough, so don't make it tougher by being too critical of yourself. Take breaks when you need them, acknowledge that you're a human being who will make mistakes, and don't be afraid to seek support.

Chapter 5: Control and Other Good Business Practices for Self-Discipline

In the last chapter, we'll talk about something you probably didn't expect to read in a book about self-discipline for writers. Yet, this one thing influences to a great degree your chances of becoming a prolific, disciplined writer.

I'm talking about the power of control and other business practices to help you enjoy a flourishing writing career. Let's talk about control first, the most important business practice, and then we'll cover other ways to build a more resilient writing business.

Historically, control is something that we writers had to cede by default to a publishing house. Writers had to find an agent or beg the publishers themselves to give them a chance. Then they had to subjugate themselves to the standards developed by publishers—including standard page counts, the type of a story you could tell, the type of characters you could have in your book and the type of ideas you could share.

It was publishers who decided how often authors could publish a new book. Stephen King himself was forced to use a pen name—Richard Bachman—just so he could publish more often, because publishers thought that the public wouldn't accept more than one book per year coming from the same author.[24] Looking back, the notion is so ridiculous it's unbelievable—if you have a favorite author, you want them to write as much as they can, don't you?

Some writers are still dependent on agents and publishing houses. If their book isn't to the liking of one of the gatekeepers, tough luck. Even if it is, most publishing houses spend little, if any, money promoting their new authors and are quick to write off losses.

The old system was—and still is—so unfair to authors that I admire those who have succeeded under it even more. Fortunately, today we have a choice to self-publish. It's by far the best decision you can make to increase your odds of success.

Empower Yourself

According to research, autonomy at the workplace is key for job satisfaction and well-being.[25] The ability to make your own decisions, contribute ideas, operate without a micromanaging boss, and determine your own responsibilities makes you a better worker.

This is also probably one of the reasons why you are or want to be a professional writer: you want autonomy, freedom, and flexibility. Self-publishing gives you that autonomy—while working for a traditional publisher is akin to exchanging one boss for another.

What does it all have to do with self-discipline, you might wonder?

For starters, as research suggests, more autonomy makes you more satisfied with your job. This indirectly affects how resilient you'll be while growing your writing career. It's easier to keep going if you're happier and have control over your destiny. You have little control when you rely on gatekeepers and luck to get on the radar of a big publisher.

Moreover, traditional publishing—for a great majority of authors (some rare exceptions exist)—is just a bad financial deal.

As a self-published author, you receive up to 70% from e-book royalties, or even up to 95% if you sell digital books through your own website, and up to 45% from physical copies. As a traditional author, you're lucky to get 25% from e-book royalties and 10% from physical copies. That's after the publisher recoups your advance, which might never happen.

Are there any benefits of traditional publishing over self-publishing? Of course there are. Some authors do better when they have an in-house editor who pushes them to meet deadlines. Some writers don't want to busy themselves with anything else but writing. Some are celebrities, with major publishers fighting over the rights to their books, offering lucrative contracts and a big marketing push.

However, for those authors who want to write and publish consistently without any limits on their creativity and without artificial ceilings on their productivity, self-publishing is the way to go.

Control empowers you. As a self-published author, you have complete control over your career as a writer. Any success (or failure) depends largely on you.

As bestselling self-published author Hugh Howey once said, "With self-publishing you don't waste your time trying to get published, which can take years of query letters and agenting, and all this stuff. You go straight to the real gatekeepers, which are the readers. If they respond favorably and you have sales, you can leverage that into a writing career. If they don't, you write the next thing. Either way you're not spending your time trying to get published, you're spending your time writing the next work."[26]

Control encourages you. Since you get a much larger share of profits, you have a strong incentive to do your best and keep going.

Control makes you sleep better at night. You're your own publisher, so there's no risk that you'll dump yourself overnight because you no longer fit your publisher's portfolio.

Entrepreneur and investor Lori Greiner of the reality TV show Shark Tank fame once said that entrepreneurs are willing to work 80 hours a week to avoid working 40 hours a week. The main reason why they're willing and capable of doing so is the control they have as their own bosses. You too can benefit from this superpower—just choose self-publishing as your business model.

5 Good Business Practices for More Self-Discipline

Self-publishing isn't the only way to give yourself better odds of success. In addition to fully owning your publishing business, it pays to engage in a few other good business practices to strengthen your foundations. This will help you better withstand any unforeseeable circumstances that could otherwise destroy your motivation and self-discipline to keep writing. Let's discuss some suggestions how you can accomplish it.

1. Give Yourself the Best Chance of Success

The publishing world is getting more and more competitive. If you want to accomplish the results you're after—such as a stable, professional writing career—you can't do it in a half-hearted way.

I've seen countless independent authors who could provide a lot of value to their readers, but unknowingly sabotage their results. They do it through a variety of ways, with some of the most common being:

1. Entitlement

No matter how skilled you are—or any other writer, for that matter—you don't simply *deserve* your readers' attention.

A lot of writers mistakenly believe that the world revolves around their work and that they don't have to understand the market in which they operate. As a result, they publish books nobody cares about—and then complain that it's impossible to succeed as a writer.

We discussed how to research your market. We didn't talk about it just for fun. If you don't write to market, you'll making things unnecessarily hard for yourself.

As writers, we need to gain the attention of our readers. We serve them, not the other way around. If you don't provide the books they want to read, you're setting yourself up for failure.

2. Skimping on a book cover

After entitlement, this is the number one sin, and the number one reason why books fail.

Readers do judge books by their covers, and if a cover is amateurish, the content doesn't matter. You've lost them with your bad first impression.

Your cover should never be an afterthought: research what type of a cover performs best in your niche or genre and make sure that your own cover reflects the best practices. Otherwise all of the effort invested in your book will be for naught.

3. Skimping on editing

Books that weren't properly edited can sometimes succeed thanks to their great content, but if you're exerting so much self-discipline to write your book, why not increase your odds of success by hiring an editor to polish your book?

If you can't afford a professional editor yet, at least use free online tools like Grammarly to make sure that your book doesn't have countless typos, grammar mistakes, or sentences that are difficult to understand.

4. Ignoring marketing

A lot of authors expect their books to sell without any promotional activities. Then they're disappointed that they didn't manage to sell even a single copy.

Before you launch your book, find some advance readers and ask them to post their honest review when your book goes live. To kickstart sales, increase visibility, and generate word of mouth, buy ads on book promo sites (google "book promo sites" and you'll find a lot of great services). Spread the word on any relevant site that your target readers frequent.

If you don't market your books, your chances of success are slim to none. Nothing kills the willingness to keep going more than spending months on your book only to see a big fat zero in your sales reports.

5. Not being in it for the long term

Barring some rare exceptions, no author succeeds with one book alone. It takes a long-term approach and consistent writing to succeed. If you expect to win big with your first novel, you're bound to get discouraged, potentially so much that you'll give up writing.

Prioritize the process over the event. It's about consistently writing new books to increase the odds that one of them takes off and boosts the rest of your catalog.

Promise yourself that you'll keep going for as long as it's necessary. You'll eventually fail your way to success.

2. Build Multiple Streams of Income

Today's market is largely controlled by Amazon, which, as we've already covered, has a 40% share in print books, and a staggering 83% in e-book sales. Many authors enroll their books in the Amazon's KDP Select program which offers some benefits (like the book being available in Kindle Unlimited, a program allowing customers to borrow books) in exchange for exclusivity.

I'm a loyal Amazon customer and am beyond grateful for the company's contributions to the world of self-publishing, which wouldn't exist in today's shape without it. However, I don't think it's wise to rely entirely on Amazon. If you became a professional writer so that you could become your own boss, it makes little sense for your writing business to rely on one company, doesn't it?

Granted, given the market share of Amazon, it's difficult to properly diversify your writing business. However, even a few smaller streams of income outside of Amazon go a long way toward increasing your control over the business. In addition to that, you'll sleep better at night—and probably work harder, too—knowing that you've reinforced the foundations of your business.

The first option to build multiple streams of income is to *go wide*, which means distributing your books on other platforms beyond Amazon. This includes retailers like iTunes, Barnes & Noble,

Google Play, Kobo, and in the case of physical copies, IngramSpark.

The decision to go wide depends on how prevalent KDP Select is in your genre. In some genres or niches not including your book in the Kindle Unlimited library means dramatically reduced visibility. In others, readers prefer to buy books over borrowing them so the benefits of the program aren't worth losing the ability to distribute your books on other platforms.

The second option is to sell your books through your own site. This is easier for non-fiction authors than fiction writers as it's common to sell how-to e-books through a website.

Non-fiction writers can also build a separate income stream by becoming public speakers, building a blog in their niche, or collaborating with businesses selling products or services related to their books.

Fiction writers have a possibility of selling the movie, TV show, or comic rights to their stories. Let's be real here: the odds are slim, but it's still another possible separate income stream worth investigating.

Another option is to translate your books into other languages. In some markets Amazon isn't the dominating player, plus the competition isn't as strong, so you can increase your share of non-Amazon revenue without much additional work.

Based on my experience, the most lucrative languages include Spanish, German, French, Italian, and Portuguese. Traditional publishers might be useful if you want to publish your books in the markets a self-published author can't access easily, such as China.

Lastly, offer your books in multiple formats. You'll increase your earnings, often with little work on your part. Expanding into different formats takes little time compared to writing a book, but it can have a dramatic impact on your sales.

For example, if you hire a professional voiceover artist, producing your audiobook takes only a few hours you need to spend reviewing the final product.

Reformatting your book to sell it as a paperback or hardcover also takes little time. It lets you reach a different group of readers who prefer physical copies over e-books or audiobooks.

You owe it to yourself—and your readers—to make your book available in as many formats as possible.

Treat your writing career as a business, because that's what it is. The more successful it is, the easier it is to keep going and producing great work consistently.

3. Have a Direct Communication Channel With Your Readers

Another aspect of control that will boost your income *and* your self-discipline is creating a newsletter for your readers. It's a great business practice because you're gaining a direct communication channel with your customers. This helps you have more control, as you can sell your products directly to your readers.

Without your own newsletter, there'll always be a middleman between you and your readers. No book retailer shares reader information with their authors, so you have no idea who your readers are. It's also difficult to let them know about your new releases in advance.

Can you replace an old-fashioned newsletter with social media? Not really. Your social media page isn't really yours. Various algorithms influence how many people will read your updates (hint: very few) and the platform can delete your account for violating some obscure rule. Social media might be useful to some authors as a marketing tool, but it's not the best way to establish a direct communication channel with the readers.

Another benefit of a newsletter is the relationship you build with your readers. Email is the most intimate form of written online communication. Whenever you feel discouraged, you can reach out to your audience to get some personal feedback.

Hearing back from your readers is one of the most powerful self-discipline boosters. It's easy to forget that there are people reading your books, impatiently waiting for your new release. Getting just a single email from one such person can rebuild your motivation instantly.

I'm beyond grateful to my newsletter subscribers who review my books, help me promote my new releases, give me new ideas for books or just support me by reading and responding to my emails with their encouragement. The sooner you start your own newsletter, the better for you as an author and for your self-publishing business.

You can set up your own newsletter with a variety of newsletter services such as Mailchimp, AWeber, GetResponse, ConstantContact, or ConvertKit. To encourage your readers to sign up for your list, include in your books a quick note with a link to the newsletter, ideally offering a gift for signing up—a free book, some additional resources, a free email course, etc.

4. Reinvent Yourself as Needed

Writing is a universal skill. Granted, you might be better at writing fiction or non-fiction, or good at writing cozy mystery, but bad at writing thrillers.

However, the principles of writing are largely the same regardless of what you write.

You can always transition to a different genre or niche—definitely faster than from one medical profession to another or from one type of construction work to another. Moreover, you'll never know what you're good at writing—or what type of a book will take off—unless you're willing to experiment.

This means that as a writer you have a valuable skill that you can adapt to the changing market—and it pays to be willing to experiment if you aren't satisfied with your results.

It's easy to fall victim to the status quo bias, which is a preference for the current state of affairs.[27] Stuck in a specific subgenre or subniche, many authors who are reluctant to change lose creativity and enthusiasm for the job. They think that the risk of trying something new isn't worth giving up their current approach, even if it's no longer rewarding.

Don't be afraid to reinvent yourself as needed and experiment with different genres, topics, types of stories, styles of writing, target audiences, etc.

Constant evolution will keep things exciting, open up new opportunities, and help you become a better, more versatile writer.

Some things I experimented with include publishing an illustrated book, writing a book with 365 short chapters for every day of the year, and writing books about self-discipline for various audiences, including people on a diet, people who want to exercise more often, entrepreneurs, and now, writers. All of these experiments helped me improve myself as a writer and keep the process interesting.

5. Double Down on What Works Best

I'm a huge believer in the power of the 80/20 principle, also known as the Pareto principle, which states that you generate 80% of the results through 20% of the efforts.

Writing is no different than any other area in which the 80/20 principle is observed.

One or two of your books will contribute to your income more than the rest of the books combined.

Just two tasks you engage in as a writer will have a disproportionately bigger impact on your results than everything else (hint: it's writing new books and reading).

In marketing, just a couple of strategies will provide most of the results, while everything else will contribute little or won't contribute at all to your sales.

Regularly revise the common business tasks, keep track of your book sales and calculate return on your marketing strategies. When you double down on what works best, you'll get better results with less time and energy. With more resources at your disposal, you'll free up energy to become a better writer.

For example, I stay away from social media. I've experimented with it in the past and found it not only ineffective as a marketing tool, but also a big time suck. While I was busy posting updates, I could have been writing a new book, which would have provided more value to my readers and have a bigger impact on my sales.

I also regularly analyze the sales of my books to identify which topics and books resonate with readers most. This way, I have more self-discipline to write as I know that I did my best to increase my odds of success.

Learning from your own data and writing books similar to what has already performed well will help you get the most out of your writing skills. Of course, it's useful to experiment, but when you find something that works exceptionally well, it pays to double down on it and ride the wave for as long as it lasts.

Should You Quit Your Job to Have Better Odds of Success as a Writer?

Short answer: no.

It might take months, or most likely years, before you become a full-time writer. Dedicating your full energy toward writing would be ideal, but we don't live in an ideal world. An aspiring writer has to somehow make a living while pursuing their dreams.

One alternative you can consider is seeking a more flexible job. Could you discuss a remote work agreement, work from home at least once or twice a week, or at least have more flexible work hours?

Your most creative hours might clash with your work schedule. For example, if you write your best work at 8 in the morning but that's when you're usually stuck in a traffic jam on your way to work, it's going to impact your productivity a lot. If you could go to work two hours later (or not go at all and work from home), you would not only avoid the worst traffic jams, but also have time to capitalize on your most productive hours.

In the end, it depends on how seriously you treat writing. If you desperately want to become a professional writer, regaining some control over your workday is well worth it. With more flexibility, you'll probably transition to a full-time writing career sooner.

But just to reiterate: by no means I suggest quitting your job to pursue writing as your new career. It's too risky, particularly if you need to provide for your family. I'm of the belief that dedicated, disciplined writers can start to make a living from writing in a couple of years at most, but it doesn't mean that these results are guaranteed.

If writing already brings you considerable income and you could use more time and energy to grow further, quitting your job might make sense. Otherwise, think of ways to make your job more flexible. In the meantime, save aggressively so you can transition to full-time writing as soon as your career takes off.

CONTROL AND OTHER GOOD BUSINESS PRACTICES FOR SELF-DISCIPLINE: QUICK RECAP

1. Self-publishing is the best choice if you want to become a disciplined writer. With complete control over your work, you reap all the benefits of your hard work. Moreover, you're more autonomous which has been proven to increase work satisfaction—and the more you enjoy your job, the more productive you'll be.

2. Give yourself the best odds of success by taking into account the needs of your potential readers. Get a great book cover—it's how you make the crucial, first impression. Don't skimp on editing as it also affects how your readers will perceive your work. By ignoring marketing, you're setting yourself up for a failure. No matter how good your book is, it needs a push so that people can discover it and spread the word. Lastly, you can succeed as a writer only if you're in it for the long term, meaning months or years.

3. Build multiple streams of income to protect yourself from depending on just one company. The more diversified you are, the better you'll sleep at night, and the easier it will be to continue growing your writing business.

4. Regular communication with your readers will boost your self-discipline and reignite your motivation when you lose confidence in yourself. The best way to accomplish this is by setting up a newsletter for readers. Entice people to sign up by offering a valuable freebie.

5. Don't be afraid to experiment as a writer. If one thing isn't working, try something else. Don't put yourself in a cage by refusing to evolve. Constant evolution will keep things exciting, open up new opportunities, and help you become a better, more versatile writer.

6. Regularly revise your sales reports and tasks to identify what's working well and what's inefficient. By doubling down on what works and throwing away the rest, you'll have more energy for writing.

7. Unless you already have a flourishing writing career, don't quit your day job. If possible, seek more flexibility so that you can write during your most productive hours. Writing full-time is wonderful, but it takes time to build a steady income stream.

Epilogue

I promised you a short read, so it's time to say our goodbyes and get back to what we both would like to do best: writing.

I hope that you've discovered useful ideas on how to develop more self-discipline and through that, become a more successful professional writer.

Don't let your gift go to waste. Do your best to grow as a person so that you can continuously entertain or educate your readers in your very own, beautifully unique, way.

Don't forget that self-discipline starts and ends with how you care for yourself: and that includes not only health, but also how kind and understanding you are toward yourself.

Your physical and mental performance are key to writing effectively, so take time to care for your health. You can't cater to the needs of your readers well if your own needs are neglected.

Another aspect of self-care is being in tune with yourself. Self-control is often painted as a superpower of people who can push themselves no matter what happens in their lives, but in reality, self-discipline has more to do with self-empathy and self-understanding than self-guilt and self-punishment.

This has nothing to do with cheap self-help spirituality. A writer who's able to make peace with the fact that they'll make mistakes, feel lazy, fail to meet their goals, or otherwise disappoint themselves will be more likely to keep going than a writer who expects perfection of themselves and berates themselves for any shortcomings, missteps, and fruitless attempts.

Striving for perfection is noble, but remember that for *long-term* self-discipline as a writer, you need to enjoy the process. Writing is already hard enough: don't make it harder by pushing yourself too hard and punishing yourself if you fail to meet your expectations.

What will your next book be about?

Download Another Book for Free

I want to thank you for buying my book and offer you another book (just as valuable as this one): *Grit: How to Keep Going When You Want to Give Up*, completely free.

Visit the link below to receive it:

https://www.profoundselfimprovement.com/writers

In *Grit*, I'll tell you exactly how to stick to your goals, using proven methods from peak performers and science.

In addition to getting *Grit*, you'll also have an opportunity to get my new books for free, enter giveaways, and receive other valuable emails from me.

Again, here's the link to sign up:

https://www.profoundselfimprovement.com/writers

Could You Help?

I'd love to hear your opinion about my book. In the world of book publishing, there are few things more valuable than honest reviews from a wide variety of readers.

Your review will help other readers find out whether my book is for them. It will also help me reach more readers by increasing the visibility of my book.

About Martin Meadows

Martin Meadows is a bestselling personal development author, writing about self-discipline and its transformative power to help you become successful and live a more fulfilling life. With a straight-to-the point approach, he is passionate about sharing tips, habits and resources for self-improvement through a combination of science-backed research and personal experience.

Embracing self-control helped Martin overcome extreme shyness, build successful businesses, learn multiple languages, become a bestselling author, and more. As a lifelong learner, he enjoys exploring the limits of his comfort zone through often extreme experiments and adventures involving various sports and wild or exotic places.

Martin uses a pen name. It helps him focus on serving the readers through writing, without the distractions of seeking recognition. He doesn't believe in branding himself as an infallible expert (which he is not), opting instead to offer suggestions and solutions as a fellow personal growth experimenter, with all of the associated failures and successes.

You can read his books here:

https://www.amazon.com/author/martinmeadows.

---

[1] Fox, C. (2016). *Write to Market: Deliver a Book that Sells*.

[2] Shatzkin, M. (2018, January 22). A changing book business: It all seems to be flowing downhill to Amazon. Retrieved March 18, 2019, from https://www.idealog.com/blog/changing-book-business-seems-flowing-downhill-amazon/.

[3] Dovey, C. (2018, July 17). Can Reading Make You Happier? Retrieved April 7, 2019, from https://www.newyorker.com/culture/cultural-comment/can-reading-make-you-happier.

[4] Time Flies: U.S. Adults Now Spend Nearly Half a Day Interacting with Media. (2018, July 31). Retrieved March 15, 2019, from https://www.nielsen.com/us/en/insights/news/2018/time-flies-us-adults-now-spend-nearly-half-a-day-interacting-with-media.html.

[5] Ingermanson, R. (2014). *How to Write a Novel Using the Snowflake Method*. Ingermanson Communications, Inc.

[6] King, S. (2010). *On Writing: A Memoir of the Craft*. Hodder & Stoughton.

[7] Smith, A. (1776). *The Wealth of Nations*. W. Strahan and T. Cadell.

[8] Soojung-Kim Pang, A. (2016). *Rest: Why You Get More Done When You Work Less*. Basic Books.

[9] Starrett, K. (2016). *Deskbound: Standing Up to a Sitting World*. Victory Belt Publishing.

[10] Hiney, T., & MacShane, F. (Eds.) (2002). *The Raymond Chandler Papers: Selected Letters and Nonfiction 1909-1959*. Grove Press.

[11] Jackson, J. (2010, August 06). Google: 129 Million Different Books Have Been Published. Retrieved October 25, 2018 from https://www.pcworld.com/article/202803/google_129_million_different_books_have_been_published.html.

[12] Wikipedia contributors. (2018, September 22). Books published per country per year. In *Wikipedia, The Free Encyclopedia*. Retrieved October 25, 2018, from https://en.wikipedia.org/w/index.php?title=Books_published_per_country_per_year&oldid=860723272.

[13] Zhang, M. (2017, October 26). 22 lessons from Stephen King on how to be a great writer. Retrieved November 16, 2018 from https://www.independent.co.uk/arts-entertainment/books/news/stephen-king-22-lessons-creative-writing-advice-novels-short-stories-a8021511.html?fbclid=IwAR362gNr0Qe4NYy7t-h2QEnyuhvSaIY1qvlUtilXq3XJV1Z8KOhb8GTnE-M.

[14] Martin, B., Mattson, M. P., & Maudsley, S. (2006). Caloric restriction and intermittent fasting: Two potential diets for successful brain aging. *Ageing Research Reviews*, 5(3), 332-353. doi:10.1016/j.arr.2006.04.002.

[15] Davis, C. P. (n.d.). Dehydration: Symptoms, Signs, Headache, Treatment, Effects. Retrieved March 20, 2019, from https://www.emedicinehealth.com/dehydration_in_adults/article_em.htm.

[16] Camfield, D. A., Stough, C., Farrimond, J., & Scholey, A. B. (2014). Acute effects of tea constituents L-theanine, caffeine, and epigallocatechin gallate on cognitive function and mood: A systematic review and meta-analysis. *Nutrition Reviews*, 72(8), 507-522. doi:10.1111/nure.12120.

[17] Smith, A. (2002). Effects of caffeine on human behavior. *Food and Chemical Toxicology*, 40(9), 1243-1255. doi: 10.1016/S0278-6915(02)00096-0.

[18] Konnikova, M. (2017, June 19). How Caffeine Can Cramp Creativity. Retrieved March 20, 2019, from https://www.newyorker.com/tech/annals-of-technology/how-caffeine-can-cramp-creativity.

[19] Poole, R., Roderick, P., & Hayes, P. C. (2018). Coffee consumption and health: Umbrella review of meta-analyses of multiple health outcomes. *BMJ*, 359:j5024. doi:10.1136/bmj.k194.

[20] Drake, C., Roehrs, T., Shambroom, J., & Roth, T. (2013). Caffeine Effects on Sleep Taken 0, 3, or 6 Hours before Going to Bed. Journal of Clinical Sleep Medicine, 1195-1200. doi:10.5664/jcsm.3170.

[21] Dongen, H. P., Maislin, G., Mullington, J. M., & Dinges, D. F. (2003). The Cumulative Cost of Additional Wakefulness: Dose-Response Effects on Neurobehavioral Functions and Sleep Physiology From Chronic Sleep Restriction and Total Sleep Deprivation. *Sleep*, 26(2), 117-126. doi:10.1093/sleep/26.2.117.

[22] King, S. (2010). *On Writing: A Memoir of the Craft*. Hodder & Stoughton.

[23] Kanouse, D. E., & Hanson, L. (1972). Negativity in evaluations. In E. E. Jones, D. E. Kanouse, S. Valins, H. H. Kelley, R. E. Nisbett, & B. Weiner (Eds.), Attribution: Perceiving the causes of behavior. Morristown, NJ: General Learning Press.

[24] King, S. (n.d.) Frequently Asked Questions. Why did you write books as Richard Bachman? Retrieved March 21, 2019 from https://stephenking.com/faq.html.

[25] Wheatley, D. (2017). Autonomy in Paid Work and Employee Subjective Well-Being. *Work and Occupations*, 44(3), 296-328. doi:10.1177/0730888417697232.

[26] Harrison, C. (2012, November 11). Self-publishing industry explodes, brings rewards, challenges. Retrieved March 21, 2019, from https://www.miamiherald.com/latest-news/article1944481.html.

[27] Samuelson, W., & Zeckhauser, R. (1988). Status quo bias in decision making. *Journal of Risk and Uncertainty*, 1(1), 7-59. doi:10.1007/bf00055564

Printed in Great Britain
by Amazon